THE CHECKERED FLAG SERIES

WHEELS

HENRY A. BAMMAN
ROBERT J. WHITEHEAD

ILLUSTRATIONS JAMES ANDREWS

ADDISON-WESLEY PUBLISHING COMPANY
Menlo Park, California   Reading, Massachusetts   London   Don Mills, Ontario

CONTENTS

I

WHEELS FOR WHEELS

The hot rod moved ahead little by little. It rolled up to the starting line and stopped. Inside the race car, Wheels White pushed himself back in the driver's seat. He looked at the starting light. Then he looked down the track to the timing light.

"All right, *Rabbit*," Wheels said to the car. "This is a time run. Let's see how fast we can go."

Just then the starting light flashed on. Wheels pushed his foot down to the floor of the car. The hot rod jumped like a rabbit. Down went its nose. Already the car was roaring along the track. It was going at top speed.

1

The little car seemed to be flying now. The only sound was the roar of the engine. That roar was music to Wheels. It was the music of his hot rod. And the music was building and building. The car was running fast!

Wheels saw the timing light along the right side of the track.

"Go, *Rabbit*, go!" he said to the car.

The hot rod roared by the go light at top speed.

"One!" said Wheels. "Two!" he said as the car raced by another light.

All at once a red light flashed. Wheels let up on the gas. The car slowed. Wheels let it roll on down the track. His timed speed run was over.

Wheels White was a hot-rod driver. In a hot-rod race there can be many drivers and cars. But only one car at a time is on the track. Each driver in turn races his car against time. As each hot rod roars along the track, its speed is timed. The car that makes the best time wins the race.

"You made good time, *Rabbit*," said Wheels to his car. "I think we have the best time."

Wheels steered the hot rod to the left. He headed back along the side of the track. A little way ahead he could see the garage where many of the race cars were kept. There the drivers worked on the engines and kept the cars ready to race. Wheels headed for the open door of the big building.

Wheels rolled the car into the garage. He parked in the place where he always kept his hot rod. He turned off the engine and jumped from the car. He ran his hand along the top of the car, then across the words on its side— *The Rabbit.*

"That was a fast ride, *Rabbit*," Wheels said. "Keep it up!"

The car garage was a long building. From one end to the other it was lined with race cars. Here was an open hot rod with its top down. There was a big, fast race car. All about the garage floor were tires and wheels, engine parts, and cans of gas and oil. Men were working in the cars and under the cars. Above the roar of running engines, Wheels could hear the sound of music coming from a car radio.

Two men stood looking into the engine of a big race car. One of them looked up.

"What's the good word, Wheels?" he called out. "Did *The Rabbit* give you a fast ride out there?"

"My *Rabbit* ran fast, man, fast!" said Wheels. "Best car in the time race!"

The man laughed. People always laughed when Wheels was around. They laughed at his funny face with its long, pointed nose between the flashing eyes. Wheels was a big man. He rocked from side to side when he walked. People laughed at this, too. And they laughed when Wheels laughed. He was a funny man. He liked people, and they liked him.

With men who raced cars, Wheels White was tops. He knew how to drive cars. He knew how to get top speed from an engine. It was said of Wheels that when it came to racing, he came to race. At race time Wheels and his car were always ready.

All at once, above the sound of the engines, Wheels heard someone calling him.

"Wheels, come over here," the man roared.

Wheels did not have to turn around to see who was calling. Only Lindy Dark had a big voice that could be heard above the roar of the engines. Lindy had worked around race cars for a long time. He knew cars and engines inside and out. He worked off and on for many drivers, but only when he wanted to work.

Wheels walked over to Lindy. The man was standing by a big red race car. It was the *Red One*. Wheels had not seen the car before.

"What's up, Lindy?" asked Wheels. "Is there something I can do for you?"

"I'm working for Bob Light. He asked me to see you," Lindy said. "This is one of his race cars. He's going to drive it in the Rock Mountain Open Road Race. That is, he's going to if . . . ."

"If what?" asked Wheels.

"Well, he has had some trouble with the car," said Lindy. "He thought maybe you could give him a hand with it."

Wheels walked all around the long car. In an open road race the *Red One* would be something to watch.

7

Looking at the car, Wheels thought over and over of one word—speed! speed! speed!

"It looks good to me," said Wheels as he came back to Lindy. "What trouble has Bob Light been having with the car?"

"Too much trouble," said Lindy. "I think the *Red One* is jinxed."

"Jinxed?" said Wheels. "Come on, Lindy. A car can't be jinxed."

"No? Well, that's the way it seems to me," said Lindy. "It has been one thing after another with this car."

Then Lindy told Wheels about the troubles they had had with the car: a broken steering wheel, two cut tires, and a broken gas line.

Wheels thought of something and laughed. "Let's take the car out and roll it off the side of a mountain," he said. "Then the jinx and the car will be ended once and for all."

A funny look crossed Lindy's face. "How did you know?" he asked.

"Know what?" said Wheels.

"Something like that just about happened," said Lindy. "The car came close to rolling over, all right—on a speed run. Bob Light was in the car at the time!"

2

THE JINXED CAR

"What do you think would make this car roll over?" asked Wheels.

"I told you," said Lindy. "It's jinxed. When the *Red One* left here, it was running all right. But I'm not the only one who works on his car. Ask Marc...."

"You talk too much, Lindy!" came an angry voice.

Wheels and Lindy turned around. Standing behind them was a mountain of a man. Wheels had only seen the man around the garage. He did not know him.

"Wheels, this is Marc Day," said Lindy. "Marc drives the *R-80*, another one of Bob Light's cars."

Wheels put out his hand. Marc looked the other way. Wheels felt troubled. "When a man can't look you in the eye," Wheels thought to himself, "he can't be much of a man."

Marc turned to Lindy. "Where did you get that talk about a jinx?" he asked. "Why don't you say that you can't keep the car running right?"

Lindy said nothing. He just looked at Marc. Wheels felt that he had to find out what was going on.

"What's this all about?" he asked.

"I'll tell you," said Marc. "Bob Light has two race cars—this one and the *R-80* over there." He pointed to a car parked near the garage door. It was just like the *Red One*. "Bob wants to drive the *Red One* in the Rock Mountain Open Road Race, two days from now."

"And?" said Wheels.

"You know what that race is like," said Marc. "All of the cars are on the road at once. They race across open road, then up and down the mountain. The driver who gets back to the starting line ahead of the others wins. You have to have a fast car to take mountain turns with other cars right behind you."

"I know," said Wheels. "Go on."

"Bob had the car out for a run on the track," said

Marc. "He was trying to get more speed out of it. He had it almost to top speed when it started rocking from side to side. The race car almost turned over. Bob stopped it just in time."

Wheels turned to the man at his side. "Something made the car do that, Lindy," he said. "What trouble have you found?"

"Nothing," said Lindy. "I can't find a thing."

"All Lindy talks about is a jinx!" said Marc in an angry voice.

Wheels eyed the two men. Marc seemed angry all the time. All Lindy talked about was a jinx.

"Something funny is going on here," Wheels thought as he turned to look at the car.

"Let's see if we can find the trouble," he said, pulling out a flashlight. "Now, why would a car rock at top speed? Let's look at the wheels and tires."

Wheels got under the big race car and turned on his flashlight. He ran his hand over the two back tires and wheels. They seemed all right. He moved to the front of the car. He ran his hand over the inside of the left front wheel. Then he felt something. He moved his hand. A nut dropped from the wheel and rolled across the floor. The men watched it go.

"That's why the car rocked," said Wheels, pulling himself out from under the car. "That nut had not been made fast to the wheel. The wheel started moving from side to side. Just a little, then more and more. If that nut had come off when the car was racing at top speed, the wheel would have come off, too. Then . . . ." Wheels stopped talking.

"The car would have crashed," Marc went on. He looked at Lindy. "A jinx, you say? It looks to me as if . . . ." Then he stopped, turned, and walked away.

Lindy and Wheels watched him go.

"Nuts!" said Lindy, turning back to the car.

Wheels said nothing. He was thinking only about the race car now. "Lindy," he said, "get in and start up the engine."

The *Red One* was a big car—big and fast. Its big engine stood on its side in the front end of the car. The engine roared as Lindy turned on the gas. Little by little he let the engine speed build up. The sound of its roar kept building and building.

All at once oil started flying. It happened just as the engine was turning over very fast. The oil spotted the car and floor around the car. It hit Wheels who was standing over the engine.

"Close it down, Lindy," Wheels roared as he jumped back. "Close it down!"

Lindy turned off the gas and got out of the race car. When he saw Wheels, he had to laugh. Wheels was oiled from head to foot. Oil was running down his face and hands. Wheels was laughing, too.

"Why are *you* laughing?" asked Lindy.

"I hit oil!" said Wheels. "I will not have to work again." Then the two men laughed and laughed.

Wheels and Lindy took the top off the engine. The top part is called the head. Wheels looked at the rods that made the engine work. One of them had oil all over it— too much oil.

"Let's take that rod out of the engine," said Wheels. "It looks funny to me."

The two men worked over the engine.

"How long has Marc worked for Bob Light?" asked Wheels.

"Not very long," said Lindy. "Bob raced against Marc and liked what he saw."

"Is Marc a good driver?" Wheels asked.

"He's a good driver," said Lindy. "I don't think he's as good as Bob. But he knows engines."

Wheels thought about what Lindy had just said. Could Marc be the jinx? If he knew how to make cars run, then he knew how to keep them from running.

"Where was Marc each time the 'jinx' hit?" Wheels asked.

"He's always around," said Lindy, not looking up from the car.

Wheels had the rod out of the engine now. It was almost broken in two. He ran his hand over the broken place. It felt funny. But there was so much oil on the rod he could not see it very well. Wheels dropped the rod into a can of gas to get the oil off. Then he took a good, close look at the rod.

"Wheels," he said to himself, "trouble is coming this way again."

Someone had cut the rod with a saw!

3

A CLOSE CALL

"Lindy," said Wheels. "I know one thing. The *Red One* is not jinxed. This engine rod was . . . ."

"Cut it!" said Lindy. "Here comes Bob Light. You can talk to him about it."

Two men were walking into the garage. Marc Day was one of them. The other man looked like a race car driver from head to foot. His face was dark, with little laugh lines running from the corners of his eyes. Wheels had not seen Bob Light before. But he liked the looks of the man. There was something open and right about Bob's face.

"So you are Wheels White," said the man. "I'm Bob Light. I have seen you around."

Before Wheels could say a thing, the man went on. "What have you found out about my car?"

"Two things," said Wheels. "A nut came off the right front wheel. That made the car rock when you had it on the track. Just now Lindy and I found a broken rod in the engine."

"A broken rod?" said Bob. "How do you think that happened?"

Wheels saw that Marc was watching him. He started to say that someone had cut the rod in two. Then he stopped. He had too little to go on.

"I don't know. But one of the engine rods is broken in two," Wheels said. "I'll put in another part. It will not take very long."

"You know what you are doing, Wheels," said Bob Light. "After you put that rod in the engine, I would like to take the *Red One* out for a run. I want to see how the engine is working and try racing over a mountain road again. Could I talk you into going with me?"

Before Wheels could say a word, Bob went on. "Marc will go along and ride with you in the *R-80*. He and I have been trying out a two-way radio between the two cars. We would like to see how the radios work on the open road."

"Well—I don't know," said Wheels. "Where are you going? When will you be back?"

"I have a cabin in the mountains near Music Crossing," said Marc. "We thought we would drive there."

"I'll drive the *Red One*," said Bob. "You can drive the *R-80*, Wheels. Marc will work the two-way radio. We will be back after dark."

Wheels saw that Lindy had not been asked to go. Lindy had been working on Bob's car for many days. He knew the car inside and out. Now he was not asked to go along. This seemed funny to Wheels, but he said nothing about it.

"Well, I can go," said Wheels. "But I want to get this oil off me. I'll be right back."

By the time Wheels got back, Lindy had left. Bob Light was in a corner of the garage, working on a tire. Marc had the door of the *Red One* open. He seemed to be doing something to the steering wheel.

"What are you doing, Marc?" Wheels asked.

19

Marc jumped. He had not seen Wheels walk up. He looked at Wheels, his eyes flashing.

"Nothing. Nothing much," he said. With that he got out of the car, closed the door, and walked away.

Wheels watched him go. "I'm going to have to keep an eye on that man," Wheels said to himself.

For some time Wheels worked on the engine of the race car. He put the rod in place. Just as he put the head back on the engine, Bob came over.

"Is the car about ready to roll?" he asked.

"Just about," said Wheels.

"Good," said Bob. Then he called across the garage to Marc. "Is the *R-80* gassed up and ready?"

"It will be ready by the time you want to take off," Marc called back.

Wheels thought that Marc's voice sounded troubled. Was he cross and angry?

"He could be angry about my driving the *R-80*," Wheels thought. "But then how can I tell? He always seems to be angry about something."

"All right," Bob called back. "Wheels and I are going

to take one more look at the *Red One*. We will be ready to start after that."

Bob ran his eyes over the engine. "It looks good, Wheels," he said. "You know engines."

Bob walked to the back of the car. He stood looking at the back lights. All at once Wheels heard a sound that he could not place. There were many engines running in the garage. But car engines were not making the sound he heard.

"Where is that sound coming from?" he asked himself. Then something told him to look up. In the dark above, Wheels could see the walk that ran along the top of the garage. The sound was coming from that walk. It sounded as if something were rolling along the walk.

Then Wheels saw it—something moving against the dark. It was a big can, and it was rolling along the walk, right above Bob Light! Then the can was falling . . . falling . . . falling . . . .

Wheels ran fast. He left the ground and went flying into Bob Light. He crashed against the man, pushing him across the floor.

Behind them, the can crashed into the garage floor. Wheels looked back. There on the floor was a big oil can. It had broken open, and oil was running all over the floor.

Wheels got up off the floor. So did Bob. Bob's face was white. He had a little cut over his left eye. But he was all right. Then they could hear men running.

"What happened?" one man asked.

"Are you all right, Bob?" asked another.

"I'm all right," said Bob. "But if Wheels had not been here . . . ."

The men looked at the broken oil can. Bob pointed to the walk along the top of the garage. "That can of oil dropped off that walk," he said.

"Man, that was close," someone said.

"Too close," Wheels thought. "In some way someone pushed that can off the walk. But who was it?"

Wheels turned around, looking for Marc. The man was standing behind him, looking him right in the eye.

RACE UP THE MOUNTAIN

Wheels found himself in the driver's seat of the *R-80*.
At his side, Marc said nothing as he watched out the
window. In front of them, the *Red One* rolled along at a
fast speed. The *R-80* was keeping right up.

The two race cars had been making good time all along.
The men had seen only two other cars on the road. Ahead
of them Wheels could see the mountains. Before long, the
cars would be starting up the mountain road. As the day
started to get dark, Wheels turned on the car lights.

Giving the *R-80* more gas, Wheels brought his car up
behind the *Red One*. He did not get too close. That would
not be good driving.

The roar of the *R-80* engine sounded good.

"If the *Red One* runs as well as this," Wheels thought, "Bob could win the Rock Mountain race hands down."

Wheels turned to Marc. "Where is the cabin we are headed for?" he asked.

"It's up there a little way," Marc said in a cross voice. He pointed to the mountains. "Bob knows where to go."

"You don't like me, do you?" Wheels asked. "Why?"

"You are just a hot-rod driver. You just drive little cars," Marc said. "Maybe you know something about big car engines. But as a driver of a big car, you would be no good in a race."

"Is that so?" said Wheels.

"I have watched you, Wheels," Marc went on. "You think you are big time. Let me tell you something. You are nothing. You and that car you call *The Rabbit*. That's a laugh!"

Wheels wanted to be angry. But he only laughed. "I like hot rods," he said. "They have a music and a voice like no other car. But I can drive big cars, too."

He put his hand on the two-way radio. "Call Bob on this thing. Let me talk to him."

Marc turned on the radio. Then he said to Wheels, "You are on, big man."

"Bob? This is the *R-80*," Wheels said. "Would you like to try out the *Red One* right now?"

Bob's voice came over the radio. "I hear you, and we will race you!" With that the *Red One* pulled away.

Wheels put his foot to the floor of the *R-80*. The roar of the engine went up and up. The race was on!

This was why they had come to the mountains—to try out the engines and to see how well Bob could drive on a mountain road. Now Marc would find out that Wheels could drive a big car, too.

They were well into the mountains now. The cars had to slow down when they came to the S turns. The two cars rocked some as they went in and out of each turn. But they cornered well.

Little by little, Bob's car moved away from the *R-80*.

"He has too much speed for me," said Wheels.

"Put a foot in it, Wheels—if you can," Marc said. "It's not the car. It's the driver."

"Watch this, then," said Wheels.

The *Red One* had just come out of a big S turn. The *R-80* was right behind. The road ahead seemed open.

Wheels pushed his foot down on the gas and started around the *Red One*. Just then Wheels saw the lights from another car coming down the mountain road. The car was a long way off, but Wheels dropped back behind Bob's car. It was the right thing to do.

After the car went by, Wheels speeded up again. Little by little he closed in on the *Red One*. Then Wheels saw the back lights on the *Red One* flash red. Bob was slowing as he went into another turn. Wheels could see around Bob's car and the turn. The road was open again.

"Now I have him," Wheels said. He hit the gas. The *R-80* moved out around the back end of the *Red One*. Now the two cars were side by side. All at once, out of the corner of his eye, Wheels saw something move on the road. It was a rabbit. Wheels was going too fast to stop, but he could not just run down the rabbit. He thought about his hot rod, *The Rabbit*.

Wheels did what he had to do. He steered the car to the left, off the road. As the tires left the road, Wheels took his foot off the gas. He felt the front end of the race car pull more and more to the right. He turned the steering wheel to the right, too.

Then the car was turning around and around. Rocks were flying from under the wheels of the car. Wheels kept fighting the steering wheel. All at once the *R-80* stopped turning. The roar of its engine stopped, too. Wheels looked up to see the back lights of the *Red One* as it went around a turn in the road ahead.

Then Marc started laughing. "Just a hot-rod driver! That's all you are."

Wheels started the car engine. "I did the right thing," he said.

All at once the two-way radio flashed on. Marc and Wheels heard a voice. The voice sounded a long way off.

"What was that?" asked Wheels. "Turn it up!"

Marc turned up the radio. They could just hear Bob's voice. ". . . car . . . off road . . . ."

"Bob is in trouble," said Marc. "Let's get going."

Wheels was already starting the car. He turned the *R-80* about and raced up the road at top speed. As the car roared around a turn, Wheels and Marc saw the *Red One*. It was off the side of the road, its nose pushed between two rocks.

Bob was in the car. His head was back against the front seat. He was not moving. The jinx had hit again!

5

TROUBLE AT THE CABIN

The *R-80* ground to a stop. Wheels and Marc jumped out and ran to the crashed car. Wheels pulled at the door on the driver's side. It would not open. Marc could not get the other door open. It was against a big rock.

Wheels looked inside the car. Bob was not moving at all. Wheels turned on his flashlight. He could see that Bob's face was white. There was a red spot above his nose where he had hit his head on the steering wheel.

"Marc, I'm having trouble getting this door open," Wheels said. "Give me a hand."

Working side by side, the two men got the door open. They pulled Bob from the car and placed him on the ground. Each one took a turn working on the man. Before long, Bob started to come around. His head rolled from side to side. His eyes opened. "What happened?" he asked.

"All we know is that you crashed into the side of the mountain," Wheels said. He turned to Marc. "How near are we to the cabin?"

"It's just up the road a little way," said Marc.

"Good," said Wheels. "Marc, you take Bob in the *R-80* to the cabin. I'll see if I can get the *Red One* running. Give me a little time. If I can't get the car started, you will have to come back after me. How do I find the cabin?"

"You will see it just after you get to a place called Music Crossing," said Marc. "Two roads cross there. You take the road to the right. You can see the cabin from the road."

Marc and Wheels put Bob into the *R-80*. Off the two men went up the road. Wheels watched the car go, then he ran to the *Red One*. He got into the car and turned on the lights. They worked. By the light, Wheels saw that the nose and right door had been pushed in. The back window had been broken.

Wheels turned on the gas, and the car started. "Well, the engine runs," he said. "That's something."

Wheels tried to back the car out on the road. The steering wheel would not turn. He turned off the engine and jumped from the car.

Wheels got down and looked under the car. It was dark under there. He turned on his flashlight. He ran his hand up and down the steering rod and felt something pointed.

"What's this?" Wheels asked himself. He ·pulled, and a rock dropped into his hand.

"That's funny," Wheels thought. "Someone would almost have to drive a rock into that spot." Wheels stopped. He thought of something that had happened at the garage. Marc had been working around the steering wheel of the *Red One*. Could he have put the rock in there? But again, maybe the car had run over the rock on the road. If that had happened, the rock could have come flying up into the steering rod.

Wheels got back inside the car. Now he had no trouble backing the car out on the road. Then he took off up the mountain. Before long he spotted the cabin. It was just off the road. The lights were on in the cabin, and the *R-80* stood in front.

Wheels brought the *Red One* up the drive and stopped. As he got out of the car, he thought he could hear someone behind the cabin.

"Marc? Bob? Is that you?" he called out. Wheels looked around the corner of the cabin into the dark. Seeing no one, he walked to the door of the cabin and pushed it open. Bob Light was walking up and down the floor.

"How is the head, Bob?" Wheels asked.

"I'm all right now," Bob said, turning. "How is the car?"

"The back window is broken," said Wheels. "The right door and the nose are pushed in a little. But the engine sounds good. I found a rock in the steering rod. The steering wheel would not turn. That brought on the crash."

"It's something all the time," said Bob. "Lindy is right. I'm jinxed."

Wheels looked at Bob. Then he said, "You are not jinxed, Bob. I think someone is trying to keep you and the *Red One* out of the Rock Mountain race."

Bob looked at Wheels. "Why would you say a thing like that?" he asked.

Then Wheels told Bob about the things he had seen and heard. He told him what he thought about Marc. At the end, Bob's face was white.

"Marc has not been with me very long," said Bob. "But I think I know him. He is a good driver, and he is a good man."

Then he stopped. "Let's not talk about it, Wheels. Go find Marc. I'm ready to drive back to the garage."

"Are you up to driving back now?" asked Wheels.

"I have to," said Bob. "I'll have to work all day to get the car ready for the race. So let's get rolling."

Wheels looked around the cabin. "By the way, where is Marc?" he asked.

"He went out to look over the *R-80*," Bob said.

"That's funny," said Wheels. "I did not see him when I came in."

"Well, he's out there," said Bob in a cross voice.

Wheels left the cabin, pulling the door closed behind him. He looked inside the *R-80*. Marc was not there. "Now, where could he be?" Wheels asked himself. "Maybe he's working on the *Red One*."

Wheels walked over to the *Red One* and got in. He saw that the car's two-way radio was on.

"Funny," he said to himself. "I don't . . . ."

All at once Wheels knew that someone was in the back seat. As he turned part way around, something crashed into the side of his head.

CUT OFF!

Wheels opened his eyes. He was on his back on the ground. Someone was pointing a flashlight in his eyes. It was Bob.

"Wheels? Wheels, how are you?" Bob asked.

"I think I have two heads," said Wheels.

"What happened?" asked Bob.

"I got inside the *Red One*," said Wheels. "The two-way radio was on. Someone had been talking on it. And that someone was in the back seat. He hit me over the head."

Wheels stood up. "How long have I been out?"

"Not very long," Bob said. "Right after you left the cabin, I heard someone running. I came out and found you like this."

Just then the two men heard someone coming. Bob pointed his flashlight down the road. He saw Marc Day.

"What's going on?" Marc asked.

"Where have you been?" asked Bob.

"I took a walk to Music Crossing," said Marc. "I wanted to see . . . ." When Marc saw Wheels, he stopped. "What happened to you, Wheels?" he asked.

"Don't you know?" asked Wheels in an angry voice.

"Someone hit him on the head," said Bob. "By the way, where did you say you went?"

"I walked down to Music Crossing," said Marc. "I know the man there who runs the garage. I wanted to talk to him and some other people I know."

"Did you see someone running down this road?" Bob asked.

"No one," said Marc. "Say, why are you asking *me* all this?"

"Well, maybe *you* hit me on the head," said Wheels.

"Now see here," said Marc, a dark look crossing his face. "If you think . . . ."

Bob cut in. "I think the best thing to do is to get out of here. How about it, Wheels?"

"I'm ready," said Wheels.

As Bob and Wheels got into the car, Marc closed the cabin.

"I'm going to take the wheel," said Bob. "Marc can drive the *R-80*."

Bob backed the car away from the cabin. He turned it around and started down the mountain road. Wheels turned on the two-way radio.

"Is the radio all right?" asked Bob.

"It seems to be working," Wheels said.

Wheels looked back at the *R-80*. The big car, with Marc at the steering wheel, was already right behind them.

Just then Wheels and Bob heard a voice on the radio. ". . . two cars . . . stop . . . near . . . Mountain Track Road."

Then another voice said, ". . . a little way . . . see lights . . . ."

Bob looked at Wheels. "Who was that?" he asked. "I have heard that voice before."

Wheels called into the two-way radio. "Marc, is that you talking?"

"It's not me," came back Marc's voice. "I thought it was one of you."

"Well, someone has broken in on this radio, Marc," said Wheels. "Do you know that voice?"

Before Marc could say a word, Bob called out. "Watch out! There is trouble ahead on the road."

As the *Red One* roared around a turn, the men saw two cars. The cars were parked across the line, closing the road. The *Red One* could not get by.

Bob had to fight his speeding car to get it stopped. The *Red One* almost crashed into one of the cars. By the light from the *Red One*, Wheels saw that the other cars were hot rods.

One of the hot rods was red, the other white. Wheels had seen the red car before. But where? Two men were standing by the side of the red hot rod. Wheels could see two more men seated in the white car.

As the *Red One* ground to a stop, one of the men in the white hot rod got out. The other two men walked around to the side of the race car. Wheels heard the *R-80* roar to a stop behind him.

Wheels and Bob jumped out of the *Red One*.

"What's going on here?" Wheels asked.

"What are you men trying to do?" asked Bob.

"Just this!" said one of the men. With that he jumped at Bob and hit him on the head with his open hand. Another man came flying at Wheels, pushing him part way off the side of the road. The man jumped on him, dropping him to the ground. Then the two were rolling over and over.

It was dark off the side of the road. Wheels could not see much. But he could hear men running. He could hear the calls of the men who were fighting on the road above.

With little light to see by, Wheels was having trouble with the man he was fighting. The two of them were standing now, hitting each other with rights and lefts. Wheels knew his man was big. But Wheels himself was big, and he knew how to fight.

Wheels kept moving to the left, driving his man back to the road. Little by little the man was giving ground, backing up. All at once the man seemed to tire. Wheels spotted an opening. He let fly a left hand to the man's eye. Then he hit a right cross to the man's nose. The man went down. He did not move. He was out.

Just then the lights from the *Red One* went out. Wheels heard someone trying to start a car engine. Maybe it was one of the men from the hot rods. Wheels was already racing for the car.

7

THE FIGHT

Running along in the dark, Wheels came to a race car. Was it the *Red One*? The *R-80*? Wheels ran his hand along the back window. He could tell the car was the *Red One*. The window was broken.

Just then the engine started. Wheels pulled open the door of the car. The engine stopped. Someone jumped out of the car. Wheels was ready this time. He brought his right hand down behind the man's head. Wheels saw the man fall to the ground.

Wheels could hear the fighting all around. He got into the car and turned on the lights. Then Wheels saw it all.

Marc was fighting with one man. They were going at it hand to hand, head to head. Bob was standing over another man. His man was down on the ground between the two hot rods. But Wheels had eyes only for the man fighting with Marc. For all at once, Wheels knew who it was. Lindy Dark!

In a flash it came to Wheels. Lindy was the one who had been making all the trouble for them. He was the one who had been trying to keep Bob and the *Red One* out of the race. And in some way, Lindy had seen to it that other men were here on this mountain road.

Just then a voice came over the two-way radio. "Where are you, Lindy? Come in." And another voice said, ". . . keep going . . . keep going . . . almost there . . . I see a light ahead."

Wheels knew he had to move fast. More men were coming up the mountain road in front of them. He did not know how many there were. But they were already on the way.

Wheels jumped from the car and ran to where Marc and Lindy were fighting. Marc was now on the ground with Lindy standing over him. Marc had a big cut on his hand.

Wheels turned Lindy around. He looked right into Lindy's eyes.

"This is from Marc and Bob and me," Wheels said. With that he crashed a left hand into Lindy's face. The man went flying to the ground and did not get up.

Wheels pulled Marc up. Then he turned to Bob and the other man. But that fight was over, too. Bob's man was down.

"Marc, I thought you were the jinx," said Wheels. "But it turned out to be Lindy."

"I know," said Marc. "I . . . ."

"We can't talk now," Wheels cut in. "We have to get out of here fast. There are more men in cars coming up the road. I don't know how many. I heard them talking on the radio."

"How are we going to get my cars by the men coming up the road?" Bob asked.

"What if they have more cars parked across the road?" asked Marc.

"I don't know what we will do," said Wheels. "But we will have to get by them some way. Let's not just stand here. Let's go!"

47

"Marc, you ride with me," said Bob. "You can't drive with that cut hand. Wheels, you drive the *Red One*. We will be right behind you in the *R-80*. If we can get only one car by the men, I want it to be the *Red One*. If a man can do it, that man is you, Wheels."

"Come on," said Marc. "Let's go."

Bob and Marc ran for the *R-80*. Wheels started the engine of the *Red One*. He had to steer the big race car around the parked hot rods. The big car just got by the two other cars. Then down the mountain road Wheels went. Bob and Marc were right behind him in the *R-80*.

"We got moving just in time," Wheels said to himself. Ahead he could see the lights of a car coming up the dark mountain road. As the *Red One* roared around a corner, Wheels saw two men standing by another hot rod that was parked across the road. One of the men was pointing a flashlight at him.

Wheels slowed the *Red One*. But he did not stop. The car rolled ahead, just moving. Behind him, Wheels heard the *R-80* pull up. As the man pointed the flashlight into the car, Wheels turned his head away.

"Is that you, Lindy?" the man asked. "We thought you were having trouble up there. But we see that you have the two cars."

Then the man stopped. He was standing right by the car window. "Say, you are not Lindy . . . ."

All at once Wheels pushed his foot to the floor of the car. The *Red One* roared away from the man and headed right for the parked hot rod. Then Wheels cut to the right. The *Red One* ran off the side of the road. Rocks went flying. When Wheels brought the car back to the road, he was around the hot rod.

Wheels looked back. The *R-80* had made it by the men and the hot rod, too. It was racing down the road behind him.

Wheels had wanted to stop and fight. But he thought of Lindy Dark and the other men they had left behind on the mountain road. If Lindy and his men came along, there would be too many to fight. And Bob wanted Wheels to get the *Red One* back to the garage.

Looking back, Wheels could see that the hot rod had already turned around. It was right behind the *R-80*. The lights from that car and the *R-80* were flashing in his eyes. Then Wheels let the engine out. The race down the mountain was on!

8

THE END OF THE RACE

Wheels' hands closed around the steering wheel. It felt good in his hands. Wheels knew he was in for a fast ride. It was not a race that he wanted to be in. But he had to go on to the end. It was a race he had to win.

One S turn after another came up in the lights of his car. He took them all fast. Too fast. But there was no slowing down now. Wheels saw the lights from Bob's car flashing up and down in his window. And behind the *R-80* he could hear the angry roar of the hot rod coming on and on.

Wheels went into a big S turn. When he came out of it, there was a slow car on the road ahead of him. Wheels eyed it.

"Can I get around it?" he asked himself. "I have to give it a try."

The driver in the car ahead slowed for a turn. Wheels pulled out and took the *Red One* to the left side of the road. He roared up to the car in the turn. The back end of the *Red One* started to pull to the left. Wheels turned the steering wheel a little to the left, too. The car was now lined up with the road again.

"Now!" said Wheels, pushing down on the gas. All at once it felt as if a big hand were pushing the race car. Its speed went up and up and up. Then Wheels was by the other car, and it was falling away behind him. He brought the *Red One* back to the right side of the road.

Wheels looked back. Bob in the *R-80* had made it around the slow car, too. But so had the hot rod. The car had speed. It was a little car, riding very close to the ground. It was not having much trouble taking the turns. Little by little it was moving up on Bob and Marc in the *R-80*.

The *Red One* roared around another turn in the mountain road. As it did so, the car's lights flashed over something in the road just ahead. There were two rocks as big as car tires! They had rolled down the side of the mountain. One rock had rolled to a stop on the white line. The other one was standing near the side of the road.

Wheels knew there was no time to nose around the two rocks. They were too big. The *R-80* and the hot rod were too close.

There was an opening between the rocks. But could the *Red One* get between them and not crash? Wheels did not have time to think much about it. His car was going too fast.

"Here we go," Wheels said to himself as he steered right for the opening.

The nose of the car seemed to jump at the spot between the rocks. It seemed to Wheels that the tires had left the ground. The lights on the car made the rocks look big— Big—BIG! Then the *Red One* was out in the open again, the rocks falling away behind.

Looking back, Wheels saw that the *R-80* had made it, too. But the hot rod did not.

Wheels saw the lights on the hot rod turn away. Then all at once the lights went out. The driver had tried to go around the rocks and had crashed into the side of the mountain.

"You can win the race in this car, Bob," Wheels was saying. "It's the best!"

The men had worked on the car all day. They were tired. But the car was ready to race. There was not a spot on it.

"I'm going all out to win the race," said Bob. "But if you had not been around, Wheels . . . ."

"We did have trouble here and there," Wheels laughed.

Marc put out his hand. "I want to tell you something, Wheels. You opened my eyes about hot-rod drivers. The driving you did coming down the mountain was as good as I have seen. You *can* drive big cars. I know it now!"

"I just can't get over what Lindy did," Bob said.

"I know," said Wheels. "But he did not do it all. I just had a call from Music Crossing. Lindy worked that nut off the wheel, cut the rod on the engine, and dropped that can of oil from the top of the garage. But he had nothing to do with the rock in the steering wheel that made you crash. That just happened."

Marc cut in. "But who hit you on the head at the cabin?"

"One of Lindy's men," said Wheels. "Lindy knew we were going up to the cabin. He had one of his men get there before we did to watch what was going on. He was calling Lindy on the two-way radio when I came out of the cabin. That's when I got hit!"

"Now I see," said Marc. "They had a radio, too."

"Right," said Wheels. "They were the ones we heard talking. Lindy and his men were going to stop the *Red One* and the *R-80*, then push them off the mountain. But Lindy's car radios were not working right. So they could not close in all at once."

"What did Lindy think he would get out of it?" Bob asked.

"Some men told him they would give him a race car," said Wheels. "All he had to do was stop you from being in the Rock Mountain race. Lindy was tired of working on other people's cars. He wanted to be a driver."

"What will happen now to Lindy and his men?" asked Marc.

"Lindy and his men have been put away," said Wheels. Then he laughed. "I don't have to tell you where!"

"So Lindy was the jinx after all," said Bob.

"In a way he was," said Wheels. "But there is no jinx in racing. You can win a race if you are a good driver and have a fast car. You are a good driver, Bob, and you have a fast car here. Why, it's almost as fast as another car in the garage."

Wheels put out his hand and ran it along the side of a hot rod parked close by. On the side of the car were the words *The Rabbit*.

EXERCISES

Chapter One
WHEELS FOR WHEELS

PICK A WINNER

Choose the right ending for each sentence.

1. When the red light flashed, Wheels
   a) pushed his foot to the floor.
   b) let up on the gas.
   c) said, "Go, *Rabbit*, go!"

2. In a hot-rod race
   a) there are many cars on the track.
   b) cars race against each other on the track.
   c) only one car at a time is on the track.

3. Wheels White was tops with other drivers because
   a) he only worked when he wanted to work.
   b) he and his car were always ready at race time.
   c) he always won his race.

4. Lindy thought the *Red One* was jinxed because
   a) it had never won a race.
   b) it was too small for the open road race.
   c) so many things had happened to the car.

5. When Lindy called to Wheels,
   a) he wanted Wheels to drive the *Red One*.
   b) he wanted Wheels to look at the *Red One*.
   c) he wanted to find out about *The Rabbit*.

How Sharp Are You?

Find the wrong word in each sentence. Change the word to make the sentence right.

1. Bob Light was going to drive one of his race cars in the Rock Mountain Open Track Race.
2. People always laughed at Wheels' funny face with its short, pointed nose.
3. Above the whisper of the running engines, Wheels could hear the sound of music.
4. Wheels White was tops with the other drivers because he was never ready at race time.

Who Is Who?

Name the person each sentence tells about.

1. He owned the *Red One*.
2. He knew cars and engines inside and out.
3. He liked people and they liked him.
4. He thought the *Red One* was jinxed.
5. He was a hot-rod driver.

Same or Different?

Say the words below. Use each one in a sentence. Are the words in each pair the same or different?

> flashed—glowed
> roars—whispers
> jinx—spell
> ready—prepared

What Do You Think?

1. Why, do you think, did Lindy have a funny look on his face when Wheels said, "Let's take the car out and roll it off the mountain"?
2. What do you think there was about the little car that caused Wheels to call it the *Rabbit*?
3. How do you think that Lindy and Wheels are alike? In what ways are they different?

Have You Heard?

The word *jinx* comes from a Greek word *inyx*, which meant a certain kind of bird. Look for the word *jinx* in your dictionary. How did a word for a bird come to mean what it does today?

Chapter Two
THE JINXED CAR

Choose the right ending for each sentence.

1. Lindy said that the *R-80*
   a) was Marc Day's car.
   b) was his hot rod.
   c) was another one of Bob Light's cars.

2. When Wheels put out his hand to Marc,
   a) the two men shook hands.
   b) Marc looked the other way.
   c) Marc turned and walked away.

3. In the open road race
   a) there are only two cars on the road at one time.
   b) each car races by itself.
   c) all of the cars are on the road at once.

4. The *Red One* had rocked from side to side because
   a) a nut had not been made fast to the wheel.
   b) Bob drove the car too fast.
   c) a rod had oil on it.

5. Wheels took the rod out of the *Red One*
   a) to make the car run better.
   b) to see why the oil had started flying.
   c) to show Marc that the car was jinxed.

How Sharp Are You?

Find the wrong part in each sentence. Change the part to make the sentence right.

1. The *Red One* started rocking from side to side because a rod had oil on it.
2. The oil started flying because a nut had not been made fast to the wheel.
3. The *Red One* was a little car—little and fast.
4. The big engine of the *Red One* stood on its side in the back end of the car.

Who Is Who?

Name the person each sentence tells about.

1. He drove the *R-80,* another one of Bob Light's cars.
2. He was driving the *Red One* when it started rocking from side to side.
3. He was oiled from head to foot.
4. He took the rod out of the engine.
5. He talked about a jinx on the *Red One.*

Same or Different?

In this story there are words that are used to mean a special thing. Here are five of them. Can you think of how these words may be used to mean something different?

rod   nut   rock   head   run

1. What did Marc mean when he said, "A jinx you say? It looks to me as if . . . ."?
2. Why did Wheels look at the rods in the engine?
3. What did Wheels mean when he said, "I've hit oil! I will not have to work again!"?
4. What things in the story tell you about the kind of person that Marc Day is?

HAVE YOU HEARD?

Sometimes people say, "That's a whale of a story," or "He's a mouse of a man." In the fourth paragraph of this chapter, see if you can find the words that tell how Marc looked when Wheels saw him. Can you think of other sayings like these?

Chapter Three
A CLOSE CALL

PICK A WINNER

Choose the right ending for each sentence.

1. When Bob Light met Wheels,
   a) he had met Wheels before.
   b) he had not met Wheels before.
   c) he had seen Wheels around before.

2. Wheels did not tell Bob that the rod had been cut because
   a) he was afraid Marc would hear him.
   b) he did not think that Bob would believe him.
   c) he was not sure he knew enough to talk about it.

3. Bob wanted Wheels to drive the *R-80* because
   a) Marc could work the two-way radio.
   b) he wanted to see if Wheels could drive a big car.
   c) he did not want Lindy to drive.

4. Wheels first knew about the oil can when
   a) he heard the other men shout.
   b) he heard a sound that was not like an engine sound.
   c) he saw the can falling.

5. When the big oil can fell, Wheels thought
   a) that Marc had pushed the can off the walk.
   b) that Lindy had pushed the can off the walk.
   c) that someone else had pushed the can off the walk.

How Sharp Are You?

Find the wrong part in each sentence. Change the part to make the sentence right.

1. Wheels started to say that Marc had cut the rod in two.
2. "Lindy," said Wheels. "I know one thing. The *Red One* is jinxed."
3. "I'll drive the *R-80*," said Bob. "You can drive the *Red One*, Wheels."
4. After the oil can fell, Wheels looked for Lindy.

Who Is Who?

Name the person who said each of the sentences below.

1. "It looks good, Wheels. You know engines."
2. "Just now Lindy and I found a broken rod in the engine."
3. "It will be ready by the time you want to take off."
4. "I have a cabin in the mountains near Music Crossing."

Same or Different?

For each word below, give another word that sounds the same but means something different. The first two have been done for you.

know	no	seen	_____
knot	not	some	_____
here	_____	so	_____

What Do You Think?

1. How did Wheels know that the *Red One* was not jinxed?
2. Why, do you think, did Marc jump when Wheels found him doing something to the steering wheel?
3. How do you know that Marc could not have pushed the oil can off the high walk?
4. Why did Bob want to take the *Red One* out for a run?

Have You Heard?

Is there a difference between a *motor* and an *engine*? Look up both words in your dictionary. Then decide which word you would use when you speak of: a train, a boat, a saw, an airplane, a ship.

Chapter Four

RACE UP THE MOUNTAIN

PICK A WINNER

Choose the right ending for each sentence.

1. Wheels did not bring the *R-80* too close to the *Red One* because
   a) the light was bad and he could not see.
   b) that would not be good driving.
   c) Marc was watching him.
2. Marc did not like Wheels because
   a) he thought Wheels could not drive a big car.
   b) he thought Wheels did not know anything about big car engines.
   c) he was afraid *The Rabbit* could win the race.
3. The men had come to the mountains to try out the engines and
   a) to see how well Wheels could drive.
   b) to see how well Bob could drive on a mountain road.
   c) to see how fast the *Red One* could go.
4. Wheels pulled the *R-80* off the road when
   a) he saw the lights of another car coming.
   b) something happened to the steering wheel.
   c) a rabbit moved on the road.
5. Marc knew Bob was in trouble when
   a) he heard the *Red One* go off the road.
   b) he heard Bob's voice on the radio.
   c) he saw the *Red One* with its nose pushed between two rocks.

How Sharp Are You?

Find the wrong part in each sentence. Change the part to make the sentence right.

1. "Put a foot in it, Wheels—if you can," Marc said. "It's not the driver. It's the car."
2. When Wheels saw the lights of another car coming down the mountain, he shot ahead of Bob's car.
3. Wheels felt the car pull to the right. He turned the wheel to the left.
4. Bob was in the car. He was moving around, trying to get out.

Who Is Who?

Name the person who said each of the sentences below.

1. "Just a hot-rod driver! That's all you are."
2. "...car...off road...."
3. "I like hot rods," he said. "They have a music and a voice like no other car."
4. "I hear you, and we will race you."

Same or Different?

Each group of words on the left means about the same as a group on the right. Can you match them?

started to get dark	nothing ahead
win hands down	with no trouble
put a foot in it	as night came
road was open	step on the gas

What Do You Think?

1. Why was Marc cross with Wheels?
2. Why didn't Wheels stop the *R-80* on the road when he saw the rabbit?
3. What do you think caused the *Red One* to go off the road?

Have You Heard?

"The two cars rocked some as they went in and out of each turn. But they cornered well." Look up the word *corner* in your dictionary. What is the meaning of *corner* in the sentence above? Is that meaning different from what you found in the dictionary?

Chapter Five
TROUBLE AT THE CABIN

PICK A WINNER

Choose the right ending for each sentence.

1. Marc could not get the door of the *Red One* open because
   a) Bob was against the door.
   b) the door was smashed in the crash.
   c) the door was against a big rock.

2. The *Red One* crashed because
   a) it hit a big rock in the road.
   b) Bob took a turn too fast.
   c) a rock was in the steering rod.

3. While Wheels and Bob were in the cabin, Marc was
   a) out behind the cabin.
   b) looking over the *R-80.*
   c) in the *Red One.*

4. Bob had to drive back that night because
   a) he had to get ready for the race the next day.
   b) he was afraid to stay in the cabin.
   c) he was angry at Wheels and Marc.

5. Wheels knew someone was in the *Red One* when
   a) he heard someone in the back seat.
   b) he saw that the two-way radio was on.
   c) someone spoke to him in the dark.

How Sharp Are You?

Find the wrong word in each sentence. Change the word to make the sentence right.

1. Wheels could see that Bob's face was red.
2. The front window of the *Red One* had been broken.
3. Wheels found a nut in the steering rod.
4. The cabin stood to the left of Music Crossing.

Who Is Who?

Name the person each sentence tells about.

1. He took Bob in the *R-80* to the cabin.
2. He said, "Lindy is right. I'm jinxed."
3. He went out to look over the *R-80*.
4. He owned the cabin at Music Crossing.
5. He thought he heard someone behind the cabin.

Same or Different?

In each of the sentences below, one word is italicized. From the words given below each sentence, choose a word that means about the same as the italicized word.

1. Wheels *brought* the car up the drive.
   (pushed, carried, drove)

2. That's *funny*. I did not see him when I came in.
   (merry, strange, fancy)

3. Before long, he *spotted* the cabin.
   (saw, entered, left)

73

1. Why did Wheels think that Marc had put the rock in the steering rod?
2. Why was Bob cross with Wheels?
3. Who do you think hit Wheels in the *Red One*?

HAVE YOU HEARD?

Sometimes one word is made up of two other words. Can you find two words in each of the words below?

flashlight   something
someone   inside

Can you find others in the story?

Chapter Six
CUT OFF

Choose the right ending for each sentence.

1. When Wheels opened his eyes,
   a) he was lying in the *Red One*.
   b) he was back in the cabin.
   c) he was on his back on the ground.

2. Going down the mountain, Marc was
   a) working the two-way radio.
   b) riding with Bob in the *R-80*.
   c) driving the *R-80*.

3. As the *Red One* roared around a turn, the men saw
   a) two men and two cars.
   b) four men and two cars.
   c) two hot rods and four men.

4. When the *Red One* stopped,
   a) the *R-80* stopped behind.
   b) the *R-80* roared past and went down the road.
   c) the *R-80* turned off the road into the dark.

5. Wheels was in trouble with the big man because
   a) the man was bigger than Wheels.
   b) Wheels did not want to fight.
   c) Wheels could not see much in the dark.

How Sharp Are You?

Find the wrong word in each sentence. Change the word to make the sentence right.

1. Marc was on his back on the ground.
2. "I drove down to Music Crossing," said Marc.
3. Wheels could see two more men seated in the red car.
4. Wheels himself was small, and he knew how to fight.

Who Is Who?

Name the person each sentence tells about.

1. He found Wheels lying on the ground.
2. He took a walk to Music Crossing.
3. He drove the *Red One* down the mountain.
4. He rode with Bob and worked the radio.
5. He hit Bob on the head with his open hand.

Same or Different?

Sometimes words mean different things when they are used in different sentences. Read the sentences below. Are the meanings of the italicized words the same, or are they different?

Park the car in the *drive*.
Drive the car into the garage.

Little by little the man was giving *ground*.
The race car *ground* to a stop.

1. When Marc asked Wheels what had happened, why did Wheels say, "Don't you know?"
2. Where do you think Wheels had seen the red hot rod before?
3. Whose voice do you think the men heard on the two-way radio?
4. Why did the men in the hot rods stop the *Red One* and the *R-80?*

HAVE YOU HEARD?

Look at this sentence: "I'm going to take the wheel." Did he really *take* the wheel? Look at this sentence: "Bob had to fight his speeding car to get it stopped." What does the word *fight* mean in this sentence?

Chapter Seven
THE FIGHT

PICK A WINNER

Choose the right ending for each sentence.

1. Wheels knew he had come to the *Red One* when
   a) he heard the sound of the engine.
   b) he saw the car in the dark.
   c) he put his hand on the broken window.

2. When Wheels saw Marc and Lindy fighting, he knew
   a) that Lindy had caused the trouble for the *Red One*.
   b) that Marc was working with Lindy.
   c) that Lindy had come to help Bob.

3. Wheels knew that more men were coming when
   a) Lindy told him.
   b) he saw them coming up the mountain.
   c) he heard voices on the radio.

4. When he came near the man on the road, Wheels
   a) stopped the *Red One*.
   b) slowed down but did not stop.
   c) hit the gas and drove past the man.

5. Bob, Wheels, and Marc did not stop to fight the men on the road because
   a) Marc had cut his hand.
   b) Bob wanted to get the *Red One* to the garage.
   c) they were going too fast to stop.

How Sharp Are You?

Find the wrong word in each sentence. Change the word to make the sentence right.

1. Wheels could tell the car was the *R-80* when he felt the broken window.
2. Bob was fighting with Lindy Dark.
3. Wheels had to steer the *Red One* between the parked hot rods.
4. He could see the top of a car coming up the dark mountain road.

Who Is Who?

Name the person each sentence tells about.

1. He had cut his hand.
2. He drove the *Red One* down the mountain.
3. He had seen to it that other men were on the mountain.
4. He crashed his left hand into Lindy's face.
5. He drove the *R-80* behind the *Red One*.

Same or Different?

Look at the pairs of words below. Are they the same, or are they different? Use each word in a sentence.

talking—speaking
drive—steer
parked—stopped
behind—ahead

WHAT DO YOU THINK?

1. How did Wheels know that Marc had not caused trouble for the *Red One*?
2. Why did Bob want the *Red One* to go first down the mountain?
3. Why didn't Wheels stop and fight the man on the road?

HAVE YOU HEARD?

Look at this sentence: "In a flash it came to Wheels." What does *in a flash* mean in this sentence?

Chapter Eight
THE END OF THE RACE

PICK A WINNER

Choose the right ending for each sentence.

1. The little hot rod moved up on the big cars because
   a) it did not have trouble taking the turns.
   b) it was a faster car than the others.
   c) its driver was better than Marc or Bob.

2. The hot rod did not make it down the mountain because
   a) it crashed into the rocks in the road.
   b) it crashed into the side of the mountain.
   c) its lights went out and it went off the road.

3. Lindy had tried to stop the *Red One* and the *R-80* because
   a) some men had told him they would give him a race car.
   b) he did not like Bob and Marc.
   c) he wanted to drive the *Red One*.

4. Marc said that Wheels's driving
   a) was no good.
   b) needed work.
   c) was as good as he had ever seen.

5. Wheels thought that the *Red One*
   a) was the fastest car in the garage.
   b) was almost as fast as *The Rabbit*.
   c) was a better car than *The Rabbit*.

81

6. When Wheels saw the rocks on the road,
   a) he drove the *Red One* around them.
   b) he drove the *Red One* between them.
   c) he drove the *Red One* off the road.

7. Lindy's men did not close in all at once on the *R-80* and the *Red One* because
   a) their car radios were not working right.
   b) they didn't know where the *Red One* was.
   c) Lindy wanted to do the job by himself.

How Sharp Are You?

Find the wrong part in each sentence. Change the part to make the sentence right.

1. There were two big rocks as big as steering wheels.
2. The hot rod crashed into one of the rocks.
3. Marc worked the nut off the wheel.
4. Lindy was glad to work on other people's cars.

Who Is Who?

Name the person who said each of the sentences below.

1. "Why, it's almost as fast as another car in the garage."
2. "I'm going all out to win the race."
3. "You opened my eyes about hot-rod drivers."
4. "Can I get around it? I have to give it a try."
5. "But there is no jinx in racing."

SAME OR DIFFERENT?

For each of the words below, think of a word that is opposite in meaning. Use that word in a sentence.

> angry
> slow
> pushed
> tired
> ahead
> win
> opened
> nothing
> coming
> close

WHAT DO YOU THINK?

1. Why was the race down the mountain one that Wheels did not want to be in?
2. Why did Lindy want to get rid of the *Red One* and the *R-80*?
3. Where do you think Lindy and his men are now?
4. What had happened when the lights went out on the hot rod?
5. Why did Marc change his mind about Wheels as a driver?
6. Why did Wheels drive so fast down the dark mountain road?
7. How long did the men work on the *Red One* to get it ready for the race?
8. What things had Lindy Dark done to jinx the *Red One*?

HAVE YOU HEARD?

You have heard people say such things as, "He put his foot in his mouth." Did he really put his *foot* in his *mouth*? Look at this sentence: "You opened my eyes about hot-rod drivers." What does *opened my eyes* mean? Look at this sentence: "The *Red One* was out in the open again, the rocks falling away behind." What does *rocks falling away behind* mean in this sentence?

WORD LIST

Wheels uses a vocabulary of 267 different words for a total of 7,950 running words. All but 32 words, which are italicized in the list below, may be considered basic vocabulary words.

a	big	dropped	got
about	Bob		ground
above	*broken*	each	
across	brought	end	had
after	build	engine	hand
again	but	eye	happen
against	by		has
ahead		face	have
all	*cabin*	fall	he
almost	call	fast	head
along	came	felt	hear
already	can	fight	heard
always	*can't*	find	here
an	car	*flash*	*he's*
and	close	*flashlight*	him
angry	come	floor	himself
another	corner	fly	his
are	could	foot	hit
around	*crash*	for	*hot rod*
as	cross	found	how
ask	cut	from	
at		front	I
away	dark	funny	if
	day		I'll
back	did	*garage*	*I'm*
be	do	*gas*	in
been	don't	get	inside
before	door	give	into
behind	down	go	is
best	drive	good	it
between	*driver*		its

85

it's	music	ready	tell
	my	red	that
jinx		ride	*that's*
jump	near	right	the
just	no	road	them
	nose	roar	then
keep	not	rock	there
kept	nothing	*rod*	they
knew	now	roll	thing
know	nut	run	think
			this
	of	said	thought
laugh	off	saw	time
left	*oil*	say	tire
let	on	seat	to
let's	once	see	told
light	one	seemed	too
like	only	seen	took
Lindy	open	side	top
line	other	slow	*track*
little	out	so	*trouble*
long	over	some	try
look		*someone*	turn
	parked	something	two
made	part	sound	two-way
make	people	*speed*	
man	place	spot	under
many	pointed	stand	up
Marc	pull	start	
maybe	push	*steer*	very
me	put	*steering wheel*	voice
men		stood	
more	rabbit	stop	walk
mountain	race		want
move	*radio*	take	was
much	ran	talk	watch
			way

we	*what's*	who	with
well	wheel	why	word
went	when	will	work
were	where	win	would
what	white	window	you